The SITTING BULL
You Never Knew

BY JAMES LINCOLN COLLIER

Children's Press®
A Division of Scholastic Inc.
New York Toronto London Auckland Sydney
Mexico City New Delhi Hong Kong
Danbury, Connecticut

Library of Congress Cataloging-in-Publication Data

Collier, James Lincoln, 1928-
  The Sitting Bull you never knew / by James Lincoln Collier;
illustrations by Greg Copeland.
      p. cm.
Summary: Explores the childhood, character, and influential events that
shaped the life of Sitting Bull, the Sioux chief.
Includes bibliographical references and index.
  ISBN 0-516-24344-6 (lib. bdg.)   0-516-25836-2 (pbk.)
  1. Sitting Bull, 1834?-1890—Juvenile literature. 2. Dakota
Indians—Kings and rulers—Biography—Juvenile literature. 3. Hunkpapa
Indians—Kings and rulers—Biography—Juvenile literature. 4. Little Bighorn,
Battle of the, Mont., 1876—Juvenile literature. [1. Sitting Bull, 1834?-1890.
2. Dakota Indians—Biography. 3. Hunkpapa Indian—Biography. 4. Indians of
North America—Great Plains—Biography. 5. Kings, queens, rulers, etc.]
I. Copeland, Greg, ill. II. Title.
  E99.D1S6022 2003
  978.004'9752—dc21

                          2003005252

Illustrations by Greg Copeland
Book design by A. Natacha Pimentel C.

Photographs © 2003: American Museum of Natural History, 1901(6): 29; Art
Resource, NY: 16 (Field Museum of Natural History, Chicago, U.S.A.), 8, 10, 12
(National Museum of American Art, Smithsonian Institution, Washington, DC,
U.S.A.), 20, 25 (Smithsonian American Art Museum, Washington, DC, U.S.A.);
Bancroft Library, University of California, Berkeley: 23 (1963.002:0769), 31
(1963.002:1426-B), 33 (1963.002:1413-BB); Bridgeman Art Library International
Ltd., London/New York/Private Collection: 42; Corbis Images: 55 top, 55 bottom
(Stapleton Collection), cover photo, 1, 4, 53, 61, 62, 65, 68; Hulton I Archive/Getty
Images: 35, 41, 47, 69; Library of Congress: 50; State Historical Society of North
Dakota: 38 (Harper's Weekly, 10-31-1863, p.693); The Art Archive/Picture
Desk/National Archives, Washington, DC: 43, 72, 73; West Point Museum
Collection/United States Military: 57.

8 9 10 R 12 11 10   62

CONTENTS

Chapter 1

THE BOY HERO

SITTING BULL WAS THE MOST FAMOUS Indian of his time, and possibly in all American history. While he was alive he was written about again and again in American newspapers. Since his death he has been the subject of many books and stories.

Sitting Bull, showing his seriousness of purpose and his plain dress

Much of what has been said about him is myth and legend. During the height of his fame many whites considered him a savage demon, nourishing himself on the blood of whites. More recently he has been seen as a great Indian leader, a hero to his people, who tried to save the Indian way of life from destruction. But in his lifetime, many of those very tribespeople opposed him. Some thought he was foolish to resist whites: the old ways were dead, they believed, and Indians must adopt white ways. And in the end it was Indians who killed him.

In truth Sitting Bull was a more complex person than the legends make him out to be. He was a great man, certainly. However the Indians felt about his ideas, they recognized that he was one of the bravest and wisest among them. He was very generous, often wearing shabby clothes because he had given his own wealth to the poor. Yet he could be cruel in battle, and in his life killed many people, both Indians and whites. He was stubborn, again and again refusing to do what the whites wanted him to do. Yet he often changed his mind, suddenly deciding to do what he had insisted he would not do. Let us see who Sitting Bull really was.

The exact date and place of his birth are not known. Indians were less concerned with time than whites were. Whites liked to do things according to schedule; Indians did them when they felt the time for them was right. Inevitably, this caused a lot of problems between the two people.

To Sitting Bull, it wasn't very important to know exactly when he was born. We know, however, that it was in the early 1830s. The place was probably Many Caches, named for the storage pits the Indians dug there, not far from the present town of Bullhead, South Dakota, near the North Dakota border.

He was at first called Jumping Badger. Indians often changed their names. It was customary for Indian children to choose new names for themselves as they grew up. In fact, as a child Sitting Bull was known as "Slow." This was not because he was slow of mind or foot, but because from baby-hood he seemed always to think things over before acting. Hand the baby a piece of buffalo meat and he would consider it for awhile before putting it in his mouth. Through his life he would always think things over carefully before coming to a decision. His reputation for wisdom came in part from his thoughtfulness.

Slow was a Hunkpapa Sioux. The organization of Indians was fairly loose and at times confusing. At its core was the band. A band was made up of relatives—brothers, sisters, cousins, uncles, aunts, grandparents. Sometimes people not actually related by blood were adopted into a band. Bands varied in size, but usually were in the range of fifty to a hundred people. The basic loyalty of most Indians was to their band: members of a band must always look out for each other.

A Sioux village. At left, an Indian watches over the horses, the most valuable property the Sioux owned.

Several bands made up a tribe. Slow's tribe was the Hunkpapas. A tribe also varied in size, but might include several hundred people—or even several thousand. Several tribes often formed a group, at times traveling or hunting together, at other times going their separate ways. And finally, in Slow's case, many tribes made up the great Indian nation of the Sioux.

The Sioux never got together as a whole—there were too many of them spread over too much ground. However, they spoke dialects of the same language, followed many of the same religious practices, shared many myths and folkways. They saw themselves as sharing a bond. At first they did not call themselves Sioux, but Lakotas or Dakotas. However, whites called them Sioux, and in time they took the name for themselves.

The Sioux were spread widely across what are today the Dakotas, edging into the states on either side and up into Canada. Sitting Bull's Hunkpapa tribe of Sioux lived in the western part of this range, on the so-called Great Plains, a land of flat, grassy prairie broken here and there with hills, sharp cliffs, ravines. The thick grass was in some places as tall as a horse. It made excellent fodder for the millions of buffalo that ranged across these prairies.

The buffalo were at the heart of Hunkpapa life. They ate buffalo steaks, turned the skins into robes, blankets, and even trousers against the fierce winters that they suffered through each year. Buffalo sinew made their bowstrings; the hooves were boiled for glue. There was little of the buffalo that the Hunkpapas did not use.

The buffalo wandered up and down the Plains in search of water and fresh grass. Following the buffalo was the life of the Hunkpapas. They would set up their little village near a buffalo herd. The men would hunt, the women would cure the meat and work the hides into robes and blankets. Then the buffalo would move off. The women would take down the tepees (also spelled tipis); the men would round up the ponies, and off they would go, sometimes traveling several days to the next good campsite. As a baby, Slow was tied into a cradle board. When the band traveled, the cradle board was strapped onto a *travois*—a frame which was dragged along behind a horse, the baby bouncing and jouncing over the rough plains.

American Indians did not have wheeled vehicles before the coming of the Europeans. Well into the nineteenth century they continued to move their belongings, and even children, on travois dragged behind their ponies.

His mother's name was Her-Holy-Door. She has been described as a kind woman, "a jolly sort who talked a lot and made people laugh." She would live with her son for most of her life.

When Slow was old enough to be let out of the cradle board, his father and uncles began to teach him basic Indian lore. The two main occupations of Plains Indian males were hunting buffalo, antelope, and other game and making war. It was therefore critically important for Slow to learn how to ride the ponies that were central to Hunkpapa life. He must also learn to shoot arrows with speed and accuracy. He must be able to ride horseback, to hang down one side of the pony to put the pony between himself and the enemy, and to hit his target with an arrow while the pony was galloping at full speed.

Spending at least part of each day on horseback from the age of five, sometimes for hours at a stretch, riding grew to be as natural to Slow as riding a bicycle is to a modern kid. Before he was ten he had a pony of his own.

But Slow was learning more than how to ride and shoot. He was also learning the ideals all Sioux tried to live up to: bravery, fortitude, generosity, and wisdom. All of these virtues were important, but bravery came first. Not everybody could be wise, but anyone could be brave.

By the time Slow was ten he was showing his bravery and skill with bow and arrow in hunting buffalo. He later said, "When I was ten years old, I was a famous hunter. My specialty was buffalo calves. I gave the calves to the poor who had no horses." Even as a boy, Slow was following the virtue of generosity.

Buffalo were at the heart of Sioux life. From these huge animals, which once roamed the Plains in millions, they got meat, clothing, and much else. Sioux hunters were extremely skillful at bringing down buffalo while galloping on their ponies.

But of course the best way to show bravery was in war. The Indian idea of war was different from the white idea, which was originally formed in Europe. Among whites, wars were usually fought by huge armies, sometimes involving tens of thousands of men at a time. The aim of war was complete triumph over the enemy. Each war had some sort of purpose, whether it was to take over new lands, seize a major city, or remove a threatening enemy.

As odd as it may seem, Indians were less concerned with winning the battle, as long as they avoided the disgrace of a clear defeat. Instead, each warrior wanted most of all to show his own bravery and skill as a fighter. There were many ways to do this, but the most important to the Sioux was to "count coup" (pronounced *koo*.) You did this by racing in on an enemy and striking him with a coup stick—a short peeled branch with a feather or other decoration at one end. Counting coup was more important than actually killing an enemy, although there was much killing in Indian battles. You could also count coup by touching the body of an enemy one of your friends had killed. As a result, Indian battles were not planned. Few tactics were worked out; it was each man for himself. This lack of planning put the Indians at a terrible disadvantage against whites, who had much training in tactics.

These beliefs about war and generosity were only a few of the different ways of thinking between Indians and whites. At times both sides had great difficulty understanding why the other did this or that. Many of the troubles between them were because of these cultural differences.

Another such difference had to do with leadership. Among whites, kings and presidents often believed it was their right to live in grand mansions and have many servants waiting on them. Indians believed that their chiefs ought to be mainly concerned with the good of the tribe. As an example, when Slow was about ten, he went out with some other boys to practice shooting at birds. When they reached the forest they found two other boys shooting arrows at a bird perched in a tree. One of the arrows had got caught high up in the tree. The boy who had shot it offered one of his best arrows to anyone who could get it down. Slow shot a blunt arrow upward, and so good was his aim that it knocked the other boy's arrow down. Unfortunately, the arrow broke. The boy who owned it grew angry and demanded that Slow pay for it. The boys who had come with Slow disagreed, saying that Slow had only been trying to get the arrow down. But Slow, to avoid a fight, gave the angry boy his own blunt arrow. Even as a boy Slow believed it was his duty to keep peace in the band.

By the age of fourteen, Slow had developed into a strong and healthy youth. It was time for him to think about becoming a warrior. In most cases, Indian tribes had traditional enemies, usually neighboring tribes with whom they contested good hunting and camping grounds. Among the enemies of the Sioux were the Crow and the Assiniboin (pronounced uh SIHN uh boyn). These rivals did not usually make massive attacks on one another in the European fashion. Instead, small raiding parties of twenty or thirty warriors mounted surprise attacks. Sometimes these raids were meant to avenge the death of one of their band in battle.

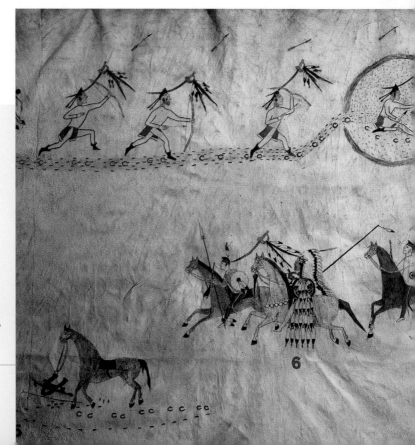

A painting made by an unknown Indian artist on an animal skin shows the Sioux fighting their enemy, the Blackfeet.

Sometimes it was to capture the enemy's ponies, which were the main type of wealth among Plains tribes. Sometimes the raid had no purpose except to allow young men to demonstrate their valor. To a young man, establishing his skill and courage in battle was all-important: until a young man had made his mark he would have trouble interesting any of the young women in the band in him.

When Slow was fourteen his father gave him a coup stick. Not long afterward, scouts from Slow's band reported that a party of Crow warriors was coming toward them. The men prepared for battle, stripping off their excess clothing, gathering their shields, bows, lances, and clubs. Crouched on their ponies, they hid behind a hill, waiting for the Crows to come in sight. Then they noticed a boy on a gray horse a little way off to one side, waiting with them. It was Slow.

The Crows came up. The older warriors waited for the signal from their leader to charge, but Slow, impatient for glory, suddenly kicked his heels into his pony and raced forward alone towards the enemy. With a shout the others followed. The Crows, taken by surprise, wheeled their horses around and began to gallop away. Slow urged his pony on. His pony was a good one, and Slow began to close ground between the last of the fleeing Crow. Suddenly the man pulled up his horse and leaped off. He fitted an arrow to his bow. But Slow, only glory on his mind, kept charging forward. Before the man could fire, Slow reached him, and whacked his arm with the coup stick. The arrow went wide, and in a minute the other warriors were there and quickly killed the Crow.

When the brief fight was over several of the Crow lay dead. The Hunkpapa warriors rode back into their village in triumph, shouting about the victory. Slow's father mounted his son on a fine horse and paraded him around the village.

In great pride he said that henceforward the boy would be known as Sitting Bull.

It is clear now that something interesting was happening to Slow—or Sitting Bull, as he was now called. Somehow he had decided that he was meant to be a leader of his tribe. It was, it seemed to him, his fate. He would show his people through his great generosity and bravery that he had the qualities of a great leader, and then he would devote his life to caring for them. Not every young person thinks this way. Most have more ordinary ambitions. But some young people do. Fourteen-year-old Sitting Bull was one of them. He was determined to be a great leader of his people.

Chapter 2

THE COMING OF THE WHITES

THE NAME SITTING BULL DID NOT REFER to the bulls we know from dairy farms and bull-fights, but to the male buffalo. When cornered, a brave and powerful bull buffalo would sit back on its haunches, ready to fight it out to the death. So, as it turned out, would it be with Sitting Bull.

George Catlin was a painter who spent much time with the Plains Indians, painting their portraits and life. Here Sioux are battling the Sauk and Fox, two tribes that had joined forces. As the picture shows, the Great Plains were not completely flat, but were broken here and there by hills.

By the time Sitting Bull was growing up the Sioux had established themselves as the most powerful and feared of the Plains Indians. They had pushed aside the Crows, the Assiniboin, and other groups, and controlled hundreds of square miles of the Plains. However, the other tribes did not accept Sioux dominance and continued to battle back. Particularly at the edges of their territory, the Sioux had to fight regularly to maintain their position of power on the Plains.

But so far, there were few whites in the area to cause problems. A tiny handful of whites had come west into the Plains and the Rocky Mountains to hunt and trap for furs, which could be sold back east for good money. Occasionally, a few missionaries appeared to preach Christianity. There were also traders in the area, who came to swap the white people's manufactured goods for furs and buffalo hides, much in demand for robes in the cold northern states back east. Indians were glad to do business with these white traders, for they wanted guns and ammunition, iron pots, steel axes, and knives, which they could not make for themselves. During Sitting Bull's boyhood, the Indians had few guns and were not very good shots in any case. But they were bit by bit getting more of them and becoming more expert in their use.

Aside from the trappers and traders, few American whites had traveled much beyond the Missouri-Mississippi line. They considered the Plains a desert, of no use for farming or cattle raising. The Indians might as well keep them.

There were a scattering of Mexicans in what is now the American Southwest and a slightly larger population of Hispanics in California. The English claimed a lot of what is now the state of Washington, but it was unsettled except for a few traders and trappers. The whole vast territory of North America from the Missouri River to the Rockies, running up into Canada and down into the southwestern desert, belonged to the Indians. On the Plains the fighting was between Indian tribes.

Albert Bierstadt was a German artist who, like Catlin, went to the Great Plains to paint Indian life and their land. In the background are the Bighorn Mountains. This was all Sioux territory.

And in these Indian battles Sitting Bull was building a reputation for daring that few could beat. The stories were many—in his lifetime Sitting Bull counted coup over sixty times. Once the Hunkpapa had raided a Crow village for ponies and were driving a considerable herd of them back to their own village at night. They knew that soon enough the Crows would be after them. As daylight was coming they saw Crow warriors charging. While one group of young warriors guarded the stolen horses, the rest turned to face the onrushing Crows.

When the Crows saw the line of determined Hunkpapa Sioux facing them, they halted, not sure what to do. Then three of the bravest Crow warriors rode forward. One charged the Hunkpapa line, counted coup, and retreated. A second charged and killed one of the Hunkpapas. At that Sitting Bull rode forward to challenge the third Crow warrior. Both he and the Crow had muskets. When Sitting Bull was well beyond his own line he leaped from his pony and charged forward on foot. The Crow also charged. As they closed in on each other, both raised their guns. The Crow fired first. The bullet slashed through Sitting Bull's shield and sliced into his left foot. But at the same time he also fired. His shot caught the Crow in the chest, who fell to the ground. Sitting Bull staggered forward on his bleeding foot and rammed his knife into the heart of the Crow. He had performed a deed of great bravery, but the wound to his foot never healed properly, and after that he always walked with a limp.

With feats like this one, Sitting Bull's reputation as a fearless warrior increased, not only among the Hunkpapas, but among all the Sioux. Enemy tribes, too, began to know about this brave and very dangerous fighter. In time the mere mention of the name Sitting Bull would make enemy warriors nervous. Inevitably, he was invited to join certain special warrior societies that existed among the Hunkpapas. Finally, in 1857, when Sitting Bull was perhaps twenty-five, he was chosen to be a chief of the Hunkpapas. He had become, at least partly, what he had set out to be as a boy. But he was still only one chief among many. He believed he was destined to be greater than that.

This painting by George Catlin shows Sioux doing a war dance. In order to be able to move easily along with the buffalo, the Plains Indians lived in tents, or tepees, which could be quickly taken down, instead of in more permanent dwellings.

We must remember that the Indians did not have the kind of formal government that we are used to today, with carefully written laws and officials to enforce them. The laws of the tribe were vague, more like guidelines than the regulations we know. The leaders did not have exact powers and duties. When a decision had to be made about war, the hunt, the time to move the village, they had to work by persuasion. Furthermore, many Indians felt free to ignore the wishes of the chiefs. Young braves, determined to find glory, often went off to fight when the chiefs didn't want them to. Then, too, sometimes the tribespeople would prefer a great fighter as a leader, rather than the wisest person.

The Hunkpapas, and the Sioux in general, were more and more coming to believe that Sitting Bull was the best chief among them. He was certainly a great warrior—there was no doubt about that. He was also very generous. He was, above all, *compassionate*—that is to say, he felt sympathy for people in trouble. He could put himself in their place more than most people did.

For example, once a raiding party of Sitting Bull's Hunkpapas chased some Assiniboin into a shallow lake. Sitting Bull counted coup twice before the Assiniboin made their way into a thick woods and escaped. As the victorious Hunkpapas gathered, Sitting Bull discovered that one of his friends had captured a thirteen-year-old Assiniboin boy. Captives expected to be killed, even to be tortured to death. Sitting Bull's friend prepared to kill the boy.

The boy, realizing he was about to die, began to cry. He turned to Sitting Bull, threw his arms around him, called him his "older brother," and begged Sitting Bull to save him. Sitting Bull felt a sudden compassion for the boy. He insisted that the boy be allowed to live. He took him home and adopted him as a younger brother. The boy grew up to be a brave and skillful warrior, known as Jumping Bull. He was with Sitting Bull the day the great chief died.

Sitting Bull had many qualities that the other Indians admired. He was a very religious, indeed, spiritual man. For the Indians, religion was not something to be practiced one day a week. It was woven through their whole lives. The Indians saw a spirit in everything—in trees, in the rain, in the sun, in animals. Sometimes during a hunt, Sitting Bull would kill a buffalo and leave it untouched for *Wakantanka*—the Great Mystery, or Great Spirit, behind everything. Usually, when something important was to be done, the tribe, or at least the chiefs, went through special rituals to get the Great Spirit on their side.

Particularly important to the Hunkpapas was the Sun Dance. Every year in June the tribe would gather for a spiritual festival, which lasted for twelve days. There were feasts, fun, good times; but there were also very serious ceremonies and rituals to be performed. Among these was the Sun Dance.

There were various ways of performing the Sun Dance, but all involved self-torture. In some cases the dancer would dance, staring at the sun, until he fell exhausted. In other cases the dancer would have a series of small cuts made in his arms and bits of flesh taken out. In yet other cases sharp sticks would be poked through the muscles of the dancer's chest or back. Weights would be hung from the sticks, and the person would dance until the muscle ripped apart and the weighted stick dropped off. Going through the Sun Dance or just observing it was a powerful emotional experience and drew the members of the tribe close to each other.

A painting of the Sun Dance by an Indian named Short Bull. Note the Indian who is leaning back. He is hanging from a pole by thongs attached to his skin.

Sitting Bull performed the Sun Dance the first time when he was preparing to become a *Wichasha Wakan*, a type of holy person. This was probably in 1856. He pushed sticks through the back and chest muscles, had cords tied to the sticks, and had himself hung in the air from a frame, dangling by the sticks pushed through his muscles. Here he danced, beseeching the Great Spirit Wakantanka to give his tribe good health and plenty of food. Sitting Bull performed the Sun Dance many times, until his back, arms, and chest were covered with scars. He did the Sun Dance not for his own advantage, but to beg Wakantanka to help the tribe. Said one close friend, "He wanted to learn to love his god and his people." Sitting Bull was clearly determined to become the great leader he felt he was destined to be.

And he would need to be great, for looming ahead was the greatest danger the Sioux had ever faced: the onrushing world of white people.

As we have seen, in Sitting Bull's youth there had been scatterings of Hispanics around the edges of the Great Plains, and a few missionaries, trappers, and traders sometimes visited. But in the main the whites kept away. Then, in 1846, the United States went to war with Mexico. The war ended with an American victory. Under the treaty ending the war the United States got from Mexico an enormous piece of land including California, the American Southwest, and more. In the same year the United States settled a border dispute with England, concerning what was called the Oregon Territory, which ended with the United States getting what is now most of Washington and Oregon. And if that were not enough, in January 1848, a massive amount of gold was discovered in California.

Back east a lot of the soil was growing thin from overuse. Moreover, immigrants were pouring in from Europe. The fertile river valleys of Oregon beckoned alluringly. The smell of California gold was even more enticing.

The best route to California went through the Great Plains. The only route to the Oregon Territory ran through Sioux country. Through the 1850s increasing numbers of wagon trains filled with gold hunters and settlers began crossing Indian territory. There would be ten, fifty, or a hundred covered wagons in a train. Each family of settlers might have a wagon or two, along with perhaps a cow, oxen, a horse. The wagons were drawn by pairs of horses or mules. Individual gold miners sometimes traveled by horseback, or in small horse-drawn carts. Some even traveled by foot, carrying their supplies on their backs or in a wheelbarrow.

Throughout the mid-nineteenth century, tens of thousands of whites traversed the Great Plains to get to California, Oregon, and other places to hunt for gold or to homestead. They always traveled in wagon trains, which had as many as fifty or a hundred wagons. These wagon trains scared off buffalo and other game, and their horses ate the grass Indians needed for their own ponies. Indian attacks on wagon trains did not happen as often as storybooks say, but they did occur.

Even though the wagon trails themselves only took up a small part of the Great Plains, tens of thousands of people, along with their livestock, cutting through the area had a great effect on the land. The overlanders, as they were often called, killed huge numbers of buffalo, antelope, and other game for food—game that was essential to the Indians for their own food. They scared off the buffalo and disrupted the habits of other animals. They camped in river valleys where the Indians were used to building their villages. They cut down the trees for their fires that the Indians needed for tepee poles, arrows, and lances.

But there was an emotional side to the arrival of masses of white strangers as well. No people like to see strangers taking over their home territory—their town, village, neighborhood, countryside. Just the fact that these strange people, with their strange ways, were coming into their lands without asking anyone's permission angered the Indians. This, they felt, was their land. What right did these newcomers have to it?

But things would get worse, rather than better. By the 1860s, when Sitting Bull was getting into his thirties, the whites were not merely traveling through Indian territory, but taking it over. In 1861 the first telegraph line was run through to California. Railroads, which had been spreading rapidly in the east for twenty years, began to push across the prairie to reach the growing population in California and the Oregon Territory.

If the wagon trains were bad for the Indians, the railroads were worse. By the 1870s, there were several lines running to the Pacific Coast. The roaring trains scared off the game, and sometimes caused prairie fires, although the fires had other causes as well. The Indians hated trains.

During the 1860s, too, cattlemen began bringing huge herds of cattle onto the Great Plains to graze. Around them grew up the legends of the cowboys and rough western towns like Dodge City and Abilene. Then, in 1871, a new process for curing buffalo hides was developed. There was suddenly a big demand for them. The great buffalo herds were rapidly killed off. At the same time, settlers discovered that it was possible to grow wheat and other crops on the Great Plains, especially with new types of plows that could cut through the tough prairie sod. In the Dakotas alone the white population jumped from a handful to 20,000 between 1868 and 1873.

Needless to say, all this activity of whites was disastrous to the Plains Indians. They could not, however, sit down and work out a general plan for dealing with the flood of whites. Old rivalries between tribes and Indian nations got in the way of coordinated resistance. Moreover, different Indians and different tribes had their own ideas about what to do. Some were ready to accept white ways. Others were determined to fight back. Sitting Bull was one of those.

For Indians, who had long been fighting each other over territory, the most natural thing was to attack the settlers, overlanders, and cattlemen coming into their country. In fact, there were far fewer attacks on whites by Indians than movies and television would have us believe. But Indians did steal livestock as they had always done from each other, did kill an occasional white who wandered away from his wagon train, did attack army outposts.

To whites this was simple murder. They could not see that the Indians believed that they were only defending their territory. In response, the U.S. government began building forts on the Great Plains, and garrisoning them with soldiers. So far as many whites were concerned, the Indians were just a nuisance interfering with the expansion and development of America. Of course, some white Americans tried to get fair treatment for the Indians, but they were a minority. So, in 1851 the U.S. government called a huge conference of chiefs from many tribes at Fort Laramie. It included Sioux, Crows,

Assiniboin, and others. At this council, government officials pressed on the Indians a treaty that set up boundaries for each tribe. Tribes were no longer supposed to fight each other and of course should not attack wagon trains. In return the soldiers in the forts would protect the Indians from white attacks, and the Indians would be paid $50,000 a year—which worked out to a dollar or so a year for each Indian.

Fort Laramie was a major strong point established by the U.S. government to protect wagon trains and white settlers. Indians sometimes attacked U.S. forts, but they were not usually able to defeat the soldiers. More often they came to the forts to trade.

There were many problems with the Fort Laramie Treaty and with the others that followed. For one thing, few of the Indians could speak English. Even though there were translators at treaty meetings, meanings of things often got confused. Many of the Indian chiefs did not really understand what they were agreeing to. And when they understood, they often realized that the terms were impossible. For example, an Indian with a hungry family to feed was not going to stop at an invisible border line when there were buffalo grazing on the other side. Nor could Indians be persuaded to stop fighting each other—the tradition was held too deeply. Furthermore, not all tribes were represented at every treaty council, and not all chiefs who were present agreed to the terms. On top of it, in many cases a chief had no right to bargain away his tribe's territory. The end result was that to a great many Indians the treaties were meaningless, and they ignored them.

What happened was inevitable. In the summer of 1854 a cow owned by a white settler was killed by some Indians. The Indians said they would pay for it, and in August "a green young army lieutenant, both ignorant and arrogant," named John Grattan decided to arrest the Indian who had killed the cow. He marched thirty men into the Indian village and demanded the man. The chief was willing to pay for the cow, but did not want to give up his tribesman, for fear that the soldiers would hang him. He refused to turn the man over. Grattan ordered his men to fire. The chief was killed. The Indians immediately charged the soldiers and killed them all.

The whites called this "The Grattan Massacre," despite the fact that Lieutenant Grattan had started the trouble. The U.S. government now built up its garrisons in the area, and in 1855 a troop of soldiers marched through Sioux territory. In an attack on an Indian village they killed women and children. The Indians and whites were now at war.

Chapter 3

WAR BREAKS OUT

THE WAR BETWEEN THE INDIANS AND THE whites was partly due to the cultural misunderstandings we have already looked at. The whites believed that their "civilized" ways were far better than Indian culture. They saw the Indians devoting much time to war instead of peace, worshipping their strange spirits rather than the Christian God of the Bible. They saw them living rough lives without the benefit of white "improvements" like factory-made clothes, railroads, steamboats, reading, and writing.

This picture shows U.S. troops attacking a Lakota Sioux village. The white soldiers had better equipment and more disciplined tactics and usually won. But sometimes the Indians prevailed.

They believed that the Indians should adopt white ways. They should give up buffalo hunting and farm instead. They should send their children to school to learn reading, writing, and arithmetic.

Many whites were quite sincere in this belief, but they failed to understand that no people readily gives up their own ways and that many Indians were prepared to fight to keep theirs.

Misunderstandings, then, were partly responsible for the Indian wars. But there was another problem. The simple truth is that whites again and again broke the very treaties they had forced the Indians to sign in the first place. A deal would be made by which the Indians were to have such-and-such a territory. Then, a few years later, the whites would decide they wanted that particular territory after all. So they would call another conference and demand that a new deal be arranged.

In general, these treaties set aside large pieces of land as "reservations" for the Indians who could be persuaded to move onto them. Here, the Indians would be given land to farm, schools for their children, Christian churches for worship. The white agents on these reservations would also supply the Indians with food and clothing until they learned to support themselves through farming. In exchange, the Indians would give up fighting and hunting.

Those Indians who did not want to come to the reservations were supposed to be allowed to live in their old ways on land left to them. But again and again whites went after such land.

Assiniboin Indians receiving their monthly ration of goods that the government had promised them when they agreed to give up their hunting life and move to the reservation. Unfortunately, many of the white agents in charge of the reservations cheated the Indians out of some of their supplies.

A typical case involved the Black Hills in Sioux territory. Sitting Bull said, "These hills are a treasure to us Indians. That is the food pack of the people and when the poor have nothing to eat we can all go there and have something to eat." The Black Hills were sacred to the Sioux.

At first the whites did not care about the Black Hills, for they were not good for farming or cattle ranching. The Sioux were given rights to them. But then gold was discovered there in 1874. Whites began filtering into the Black Hills to mine for gold. The soldiers were supposed to keep the gold miners away, but they did not try very hard to do so. In time there were thousands of miners in the Black Hills, along with ranchers selling beef and other supplies to the miners. It is not surprising that the Indians grew to distrust the whites. Sitting Bull in particular came to believe they were all liars.

Especially annoying to Sitting Bull and his tribe was Fort Buford, which the whites had built in the heart of Hunkpapa territory in 1866. Again and again Sitting Bull attacked the fort. His warriors inflicted damage and killed some soldiers, but the soldiers had cannon and plenty of rifles, and the Indians could never finally finish off the fort.

An engraving of one of the rough, tough Western towns that grew up around the mines. This is Deadwood City in the Black Hills, the land that was important to the Sioux. The street shown here would have been a sea of mud much of the time, and everything in the crude stores was very expensive.

Sitting Bull was not the only Sioux to fight the white soldiers. The Oglala chief Red Cloud was also at war with them. In December 1866, the Oglalas lured some eighty soldiers out of the fort and slaughtered them all. Among the Indians was "a brooding, mystical young Oglala warrior named Crazy Horse," who would go on to be one of the most renowned of all Indian warriors.

By now the Indians had guns and were learning how to use them well. By the late 1860s a much improved gun had come into use, the breech-loading repeating rifle. Traders were not supposed to sell these guns to the Indians, but they often did. Indian firepower increased. Nonetheless, the Indian system of warfare, based on fast raids, counting coup, and individual combat could not work against a body of well-armed, disciplined soldiers. The Indians won many battles, though, especially when they had the whites outnumbered.

The Oglala chief Red Cloud, wearing the fringed animal skin shirt typical of the time, but with white-style trousers. Indians adopted some white customs, but never fully accepted the white lifestyle.

Matters finally came to a head over the Black Hills. By the mid-1870s there were some 15,000 miners in the Black Hills. Now the U.S. government, once again breaking its own treaty, decided to let the miners stay. The Black Hills would no longer belong to the Sioux. Instead, troops would be sent against the Indians to "*whip* them into submission." The Indians were given an ultimatum: give up their old ways and come onto a reservation or soldiers would be sent against them in force.

Many Indians agreed to go onto reservations, either because they were tired of fighting, or because they believed they could not win. But many did not. Among the Sioux, probably a third were determined not to give in. In Sitting Bull's Hunkpapa tribe perhaps half remained loyal to the old ways. And it was becoming clearer and clearer to those willing to fight off the whites that Sitting Bull was their leader.

Those who saw this decided that the Sioux needed an overall chief. There had never been such

a leader. The Sioux were held together only by a common language and common beliefs and rarely acted together as a nation in war, the hunt, or anything else. Now many of the chiefs who knew Sitting Bull decided on their own to name him chief of all the Sioux. Other chiefs agreed. Most important of them was Crazy Horse. He was not a wise man, like Sitting Bull, but he was considered by many to be the greatest of all Sioux warriors.

So it was agreed. At the ceremony to make him leader, one of the chiefs said, "We have elected you as our war chief, leader of the entire Sioux nation. When you tell us to fight, we shall fight, when you tell us to make peace, we shall make peace." Sitting Bull was now what he felt he had always been fated to be: the leader of his people. He believed it was his sacred duty to save his people from the whites and preserve their old way of life. His life would be given to his people.

The American government had set a date: all the Indians would have to go to a reservation by January 31, 1876, or face the U.S. army. Once again cultural misunderstandings played a role. As we have seen, the Indians were casual about time. They did not plan to do things on exact dates, but when the time seemed ripe for them. A precise date like January 31 meant nothing to them. Even if they intended to go to a reservation, it would be when it suited them to go. At the moment a hard winter was on. The valleys were deep in snow, the temperatures sometimes down to forty below zero. The Indians had no wish to go anywhere or fight anybody, only to get through the hard winter.

But the whites had other ideas. To them an ultimatum was final. When the Indians failed to come to the reservation as ordered, troops were sent out. They came across a village of Sioux and Cheyennes camped on the bank of the Powder River. They caught the Indians at dawn. The Indians burst out of their tepees and fled as the soldiers stormed through the village on horseback, firing at Indians. The males managed finally to make a stand in ravines near thc village and drove the soldiers away.

General William Tecumseh Sherman had been one of the great heroes of the North during the Civil War. He was then sent out to pacify the Indians. Sherman believed that Indians could only be managed by force. Though there were many whites in and out of government who wanted fair treatment for Indians, the general policy was usually harsh.

The attack astonished the Indians. Not understanding what the whites meant by an ultimatum, they did not know why they had been attacked. Their village destroyed, they found shelter in Sitting Bull's village a good distance away. Now the Sioux who did not wish to go to the reservations began to gather under Sitting Bull's leadership. Crazy Horse and the Oglalas offered strong support.

Sitting Bull had said all along that he had no quarrel with the whites, *so long as they stayed out of Sioux territory*. His Indians were mainly concerned with hunting and raiding their traditional enemies, like the Crows. They had no wish to fight whites. So Sitting Bull decided that they would fight just defensive battles. They would fight whites only if attacked. Nonetheless, they would not split up into small groups as Indians often did for the hunt, but for safety would travel together in a large village. By now there had gathered three thousand people, eight hundred of them warriors.

As spring turned into summer there were plenty of buffalo for all. The people began to feel well-fed and comfortable. They felt that this large village could defend itself against soldiers. Sitting Bull decided to perform a Sun Dance to beg Wakantanka for support against whites. During the ritual he had fifty tiny pieces of flesh gouged from beneath the skin of each arm. Then he danced, staring into the sun. When he finally fainted, he had a vision of soldiers attacking the village on their horses. But they were upside down. Sitting Bull said that this meant that all the soldiers would be killed.

Within a week there was a fight. Some Sioux spotted soldiers marching toward the Rosebud River. Sitting Bull, true to his decision not to fight unless attacked, tried to hold his warriors back. But there was no holding the younger men. Off they went and caught the soldiers as they were resting, their horses unsaddled. For hours the fighting went back and forth. Sitting Bull, his arms still swollen from the Sun Dance, could not fight, but traveled up and down the lines encouraging his men. Again and again the Indians charged, only to be driven off by superior firepower. Finally, as it began to grow late in the day, the Indians pulled back and returned to their village. The soldiers marched back to their base camp. They would not venture out again until they had reinforcements.

But this had not been the great victory foretold in Sitting Bull's Sun Dance vision. He still expected that to come. His confidence increased when bunches of Indians living on the reservations began to join the village, as they often did in summer, to hunt buffalo. Now Sitting Bull had 1,800 fighting men. He was sure he could win any battle.

In search of buffalo, not soldiers, the village moved to a river called the Little Bighorn. What Sitting Bull did not know was that a commander called George Armstrong Custer was leading a regiment of 750 soldiers in search of the Sioux.

Chapter 4

THE FAMOUS BATTLE

THE INDIANS KNEW ABOUT GEORGE Armstrong Custer. He was a flamboyant man who wore his red-gold hair down to his collar. He had become a hero during the Civil War, which had ended about ten years earlier. He was much admired by many Americans as a great fighting man.

A typical Sioux encampment. Relatives usually lived in a cluster of tepees. Encampments were made near water. At left, an Indian stands watch over the ponies.

In early summer Custer led his Seventh Cavalry Regiment out into the Plains. They picked up signs of Indian campsites along the Rosebud River, and from June 22 to June 24 they worked their way up the Rosebud, following after the moving Indian village. Custer figured that the Indians were headed for the Little Bighorn. He hoped to catch them there. He assumed that if the Indians realized that a full regiment of cavalry was after them, they would break into small groups and flee. He therefore wanted to catch them by surprise so he could capture—or slaughter—the whole village. It was the first of several mistakes Custer would make.

By nightfall of June 24 Custer had come close to his quarry. He planned to rest the men on the twenty-fifth and then strike at dawn the next day. The twenty-fifth dawned hot and cloudless. He sent out scouts, who reported seeing Indians moving around the hills in the distance. There was also a faint haze over the Little Bighorn River valley—the smoke from many campfires. This, and other clues, ought to have warned Custer that the Indian village was a good deal larger than they usually were. He missed the clues. It was a second major mistake.

Now, afraid that the Sioux had spotted his troops, he decided to attack at once before the Indians could pack up and flee. In fact, the Indians were not yet aware of the troops only fifteen miles away. They were going about their ordinary daily tasks. But Custer was now on the move, and soon the

Indians discovered that he was coming toward them. Hastily the women and children were taken away into some hills to the west of the river. The Sioux warriors painted themselves for battle, found their ponies, and prepared to fight.

Now Custer made a third mistake. Instead of keeping his regiment together, he sent a battalion of men under Captain Frederick Benteen to the south to see if there were more Indians there. Then he sent another group of 175 men under Major Marcus Reno to hit the village from the south. Reno thought that Custer, with the remaining troops, would follow in support of him. Instead, Custer swung his troops into the hills along the eastern edge of the village. He was thinking that if he and Reno attacked the village from two different points he would have the Indians trapped and force them to surrender.

The colorful and determined General Custer

Reno's troops approached the village, dismounted, and began to fire—they could shoot more accurately kneeling or lying prone than on horseback. Sitting Bull, wearing only a shirt and leggings and carrying a rifle and a pistol, urged his braves into battle. They raced to the edge of the village to face Major Reno's troops. For fifteen minutes the two sides shot at each other. The soldiers ran forward in a crouch until they were only a hundred yards from the village and dropped to their stomachs to fire.

The Indians now charged them, hundreds of them against Reno's 175. Heavy fire from the soldiers forced them to veer off to the side. They swung in behind the soldiers. The soldiers, fearful of being surrounded by a much larger force, rose and ran off into a nearby stand of trees. There was a dried riverbed here at the edge of the trees. The soldiers dropped into it, forming a defensive line. Already the Indians were gaining the advantage.

Now Crazy Horse with a group of his own warriors on horseback charged forward and started once again to swing around behind the soldiers. The soldiers scrambled back into the woods until they reached a small clearing. The Indians charged in on them. The now desperate soldiers climbed onto their horses and galloped away across the Plains. The Indians chased after them on their swift ponies. They got in among the fleeing soldiers, shooting them and knocking them from their horses with tomahawks and rifles.

in kpa tan hay to kuya
Wica ktepi kin he kopi
he le owapi he ce oli to ca
Ku wapi. Wakpa a wica yapi
Wica kuyaninin to kuya
ikiye la kiska a wite yapi
tuye eto wapi.

Two paintings of the famous Battle of the Little Bighorn
by an Indian painter named Amos Bad Heart Buffalo.
At top, Indians attack soldiers riding in precise formation.
At bottom, the soldiers flee as the Indians cut them down.

The soldiers reached a river and floundered across, with the Indians still pulling them down and killing them. Across the river a little distance was a steep bluff, and on the top the soldiers assembled to make one more defensive stand. Of the original 175, less than 100 were left.

Sitting Bull, who had held himself back to see how the fighting developed, now rode forward. The women and boys of the tribe, as was the custom, were stripping the dead of their clothes and taking weapons and whatever else was of value. In some cases they mutilated the corpses of the enemy so that they would go before their ancestors in a shameful condition.

The Indians, who vastly outnumbered Reno's troops, could easily have finished them off, but this time Reno had some luck, for the Indians now spotted Custer's blue-shirted soldiers in the hills to the east of the village. The Indians turned away from Reno's troops and hastily crossed the village to face the new threat.

The fighting between Reno and the Sioux had raised a great deal of dust from the hot river valley floor. In the hills Custer could not see through the dust to follow what was going on. He was unaware that Reno had been badly beaten, nor did he realize yet how large the Indian village was. He assumed that the dust was being raised by the Indians in flight. He was wrong on that count, too. But as he led his men down from the hills he finally realized that he was in serious trouble. Hastily he sent a messenger in search of

Captain Benteen, with orders to bring his men up immediately. Then he organized his troops of about 210 men on a ridge to make a stand.

The Indians attacked. As usual, it was a disorganized attack, with each Indian looking for a single soldier to fight. Some of them swung around to the rear of the ridge, and soon Custer's little band, faced by more than one thousand warriors, was surrounded.

Another painting of the Battle of the Little Bighorn by an Indian artist, this one called White Bird. At right, a group of soldiers fire from the protection of a ravine. At left, the soldiers' horses flee as the Indians charge.

The soldiers were dismounted, kneeling or lying flat to fire, while a few men held the horses. The Indians shot at the horse-holders, and when they killed them or drove them away, panicked the horses so that they ran from the battle-field. The Indians chased them down and took from their saddlebags large amounts of ammunition they could use for their own guns. The ranks of soldiers dwindled, as they were killed by rifle fire or more frequently run down by charging Indians who clubbed them or knifed them. It was hard for any of the fighters to see through the dust. Sometimes the soldiers, out of ammunition, fought with fists, knives, or empty pistols. But it was always two or three Indians against one soldier, and the troops died rapidly. At one point forty of the soldiers, some on horseback, managed to break loose from the battle to race down the hillside. They ran through the surrounding Indians into a gully. Here they were trapped, and the Indians quickly finished them off. An hour after the battle had started it was all over. Custer and his 210 men all lay dead on the battlefield.

Meanwhile, Captain Benteen had finally come up and joined Major Reno on the flat hilltop. They could hear the firing at the other side of the village but they had no idea of what serious trouble Custer was in. With about 350 men, they formed a defensive line. The Indians surrounded them and attacked. The two sides fought inconclusively until dusk. In the morning they resumed the battle. Then word came that more soldiers were on the way. Sitting Bull was ready to leave and let the rest of the soldiers go. They had won a great victory—the greatest victory the Sioux would ever have over whites. So they packed up the village and left. Sitting Bull's vision of the upside-down soldiers had come true.

But in the long run, the victory in the Battle of the Little Bighorn proved not to have been worth it. Custer had been a popular figure among Northerners, admired by civilians and well liked by other army officers. The slaughter at Little Bighorn enraged many whites, who forgot that the Indians had been minding their own business when Custer attacked. As the leader of the Sioux, much of the blame for what became known as "Custer's Last Stand" was laid on Sitting Bull's shoulders. Many whites wanted revenge; any remaining ideas of fairness they had went out the window. Sitting Bull was their main target.

The U.S. government was now determined to put an end to the problems with the Indians for good. All Indians would be forced onto reservations, where they would have to give up their old nomadic life on the Plains. They would, instead, become farmers.

The army sent a tough, ambitious general named Nelson A. Miles onto the plains to force the rebellious Indians, especially Sitting Bull, onto reservations. Miles arranged a meeting with Sitting Bull in hopes of persuading him to take his band peacefully onto the reservation assigned to him.

Sitting Bull refused. Instead, he demanded that Miles take his troops away and leave the Indians alone to follow the buffalo as always. But Miles had his orders. He later wrote his wife a description of the now famous Sitting Bull:

> *He has a large broad head and strong features. He is a man evidently of great influence and a thinking reasoning being. . . . I think he feels that his strength is somewhat exhausted and he appeared much depressed, suffering from nervous excitement and loss of power. . . . At times he was almost inclined to accept the situation, but . . . he did not accept.*

Many of the Indians, however, had decided that they could not win. They were ready to give up and do what the white man demanded. Now Sitting Bull saw his chiefs one by one packing up and leaving for the reservations. In his heart Sitting Bull knew that he could not win. But he was determined to go on fighting.

This is one of the best-known photographs of Sitting Bull. Once again, note the simplicity of his clothes and his serious but kindly face.

Chapter 5

THE LAST OF THE SIOUX

THE REMAINDER OF SITTING BULL'S
story is sad and can be quickly told. For four years
he fought a desperate battle to hang onto Indian
ways. There was fighting with General Miles, but
his band was dwindling, and he could not win
against the soldiers. The band drifted northward.
In 1877 Crazy Horse surrendered 1,200 ponies and
117 guns and went onto the reservation. It was a
signal that the Indians were finished.

*A later picture of Sitting Bull, in the more fanciful
costume he probably wore when he was touring with
Buffalo Bill's famous show.*

But Sitting Bull would not give up. He decided to move to Canada. The Canadian government had enough problems with their own Indians and weren't eager to take in American Indians. However, they reluctantly allowed them to come, but would take no responsibility for feeding and clothing them. Sitting Bull settled in Canada with about one thousand Hunkpapas, all that was left of the tribe.

Sitting Bull himself said, "I will remain what I am until I die, a hunter, and when there are no more buffalo or other game I will send my children to hunt and live on prairie mice, for where an Indian is shut up in one place his body becomes weak."

Sitting Bull had now become a celebrity—hated by many whites but feared and admired by others. Reporters frequently tried to interview him, and sometimes there were stories about him in American newspapers. One wrote, "He has, at least, the magic sway of Mohammed over the rude war tribes that engirdle him. Everybody talks of Sitting Bull, and, whether he be a figurehead, or an idea, or an incomprehensible mystery, his present influence is undoubted. His very name is potent."

But newspaper stories could not be eaten. The buffalo, shot for their hides by whites as well as hungry Indians, were rapidly dwindling; by 1883 they would be almost gone. Food for Sitting Bull and his people was in short supply. Hungry Indians were in search of buffalo, wherever they were. Often that was across the border in the United States.

Sitting Bull became a celebrity, especially after the
Indian victory at Little Bighorn. Some thought him a
great hero, some a terrible villain. Harper's Weekly,
one of the nation's most important magazines of the
day, featured him on its cover.

Americans were angered by the Indians using Canada as a refuge from which to make raids into the United States. The Canadian government did not want to get into a quarrel with the United States. In time it was decided that Sitting Bull and his people could not stay in Canada anymore. Finally it was over. Forced out of Canada, Sitting Bull had no choice. In 1881 he gave up. Somebody who witnessed his surrender said, "Nothing but nakedness and starvation has driven this man to submission, and that not on his own account but for the sake of his children, of whom he is very fond."

At the surrender Sitting Bull was required to give up his weapons and his ponies. He would not, however, turn in his gun himself. He had one of his sons pick it up and hand it to the officer in charge. He said, "I surrender this rifle to you through my young son, whom I now desire to teach in this manner that he has become a friend of the Americans. . . . I wish it to be remembered that I was the last man of my tribe to surrender my rifle."

So the proud and heroic Sitting Bull went onto a reservation. He was determined to stay quiet, learn how to farm and enjoy life with his growing family of children and grandchildren. But his influence with the Indians, even on the reservation, remained strong. He had been their leader for many years. He was the man they looked to for advice and help. He, himself, still felt it was his duty to guide and protect them. In his heart he and his people were one. He had always sacrificed his own good for them, and he always would. For example, because he was so celebrated as almost a living myth, evil to some, a hero to others, there was great demand among whites to see him.

Sitting Bull's family and their tepee on the reservation. This picture was probably made to sell as a souvenir, perhaps in connection with the Buffalo Bill show.

A showman named William F. Cody, best known as Buffalo Bill, took him on a tour with his Wild West Show. People flocked to see Sitting Bull and demanded his autograph. He made a fair amount of money from such ventures, but typically he used it for the good of his family and his people. He himself remained poor.

This was a publicity photograph, showing Sitting Bull and Buffalo Bill Cody, made to advertise Sitting Bull's appearance with the show.

Unfortunately, his wish to help his people sometimes got him in trouble with the whites who ran the reservations. One important case involved a large piece of land that had been granted to the Indians. As ever, the whites had changed their mind about this land and were trying to force the Indians to sell it back to them at a very low price. Sitting Bull and some other chiefs tried to persuade the Indians not to give in. He even went to Washington, D.C., with a delegation to try at least to get a better price from the authorities there. The effort failed, and in time the U.S. government got the land.

Sitting Bull's effort to keep his Indians from signing away this land greatly annoyed many of the whites in charge of the reservations. There was talk about putting him in an army prison so he could not stir up the Indians against the white authorities anymore. However, the authorities were afraid that if they arrested Sitting Bull, the Indians might rise up in revolt. So they held off.

Then, in the summer of 1889, the Sioux began to hear rumors of a god come to Earth to save the Indians. So the story went, the Messiah had come in the form of a Paiute Indian named Wovoka. By following his religion and dancing a certain "Ghost Dance," the Indians would pass into a new land where there was plenty of game and no whites to bother them. Many Indians adopted the Ghost Dance religion.

The Ghost Dance spread rapidly among the Indians. Soon it came to Sitting Bull's reservation. The U.S. authorities were opposed to it, fearful that the new religion would encourage the Indians to rebel against them. They decided to squelch it.

Sitting Bull was not convinced by the Ghost Dance religion. Nonetheless, it was the job of a tribal leader to see to the happiness of his people. If his tribespeople wanted to join the Ghost Dance cult he would not try to stop them.

However, the U.S. authorities knew that Sitting Bull still had much influence with the Indians. They told him that he must speak out against the Ghost Dance. Sitting Bull refused. He told his people they could do the Ghost Dance. It hurt no one, he explained to the authorities. But the authorities were now tired of Sitting Bull's resisting them. They decided to arrest him and put him in a military prison, where he could not cause problems.

They did not want to use soldiers for the arrest, for that might end with the Ghost Dancers and the soldiers in a fight. Instead, they would send the reservation's own police force. These police were Indians who had decided to cooperate with the white authorities. Many of them were former members of Sitting Bull's tribe. He knew them. Furthermore, Sitting Bull's supporters were used to them and would not be so alarmed by seeing them come around as they would be by soldiers.

Early in the morning of December 15, 1890, forty-three reservation policemen came for Sitting Bull. They dragged him naked from his bed. At first he seemed willing to go along with them. They hurried him into his clothes. But the uproar had awakened nearby people. Indians began to gather. Some of them shouted that they would not let Sitting Bull be taken. Sitting Bull himself now began to hold back. Shots were fired. One of the policemen was hit. The police fired back. And when they saw that they might be stopped from arresting Sitting Bull, they shot him, killing him instantly. One of the greatest of all Indians had died as he had lived, resisting the white man.

The question remains, why couldn't some solution have been worked out that would have allowed the Indians to follow their old way of life? The simplest answer is the greed of whites, who constantly wanted more land. No matter what sort of treaty they signed or what promises they made, the time always came when white people wanted land they had allowed to the Indians. And they had the power to get their way.

*Indians on the reservation now used wagons
instead of travois and were learning to farm
rather than hunt for food. Most would have pre-
ferred the old life, but they had no choice but to
adopt white ways. It would be a long time before
they felt at home with their new lifestyle.*

However, there are always two sides to every question. We cannot look at the story only from the Indians' point of view. In demanding the right to live as they had always lived, Sitting Bull and other Indians were insisting that huge areas of land, amounting to tens of thousands of square miles of prairies, hills, and valleys be reserved for several thousand Indians to follow the buffalo in. On the same land millions of people could live comfortably, following the white system of farming and manufacturing. Times had changed, whites insisted. The population of the world was rapidly increasing. A new way of life had come. Some of the Indians recognized this and moved onto the reservations to learn the white culture. But Sitting Bull would not.

Still, the fact remains that during Sitting Bull's time, the whites broke nearly every promise they made to the Indians. Making matters worse, for a period, many of the reservations were run by corrupt white officials. They took for themselves a lot of the money meant to benefit the Indians and allowed their friends to dupe the Indians in one way or another. There is no question that for a long time the white authorities treated the Indians they had in their power very badly. As a result, the Indians have been a long time finding their way in American society.

Not long after moving to the reservation Sitting Bull told an interviewer, "The life of the white men is slavery. They are prisoners in towns or farms. The life my people want is a life of freedom. I have seen nothing that a white man has, houses or railways or clothing or food, that is as good as the right to move in the open country and live in our own fashion."

But it could not be. The world was moving in a different direction.

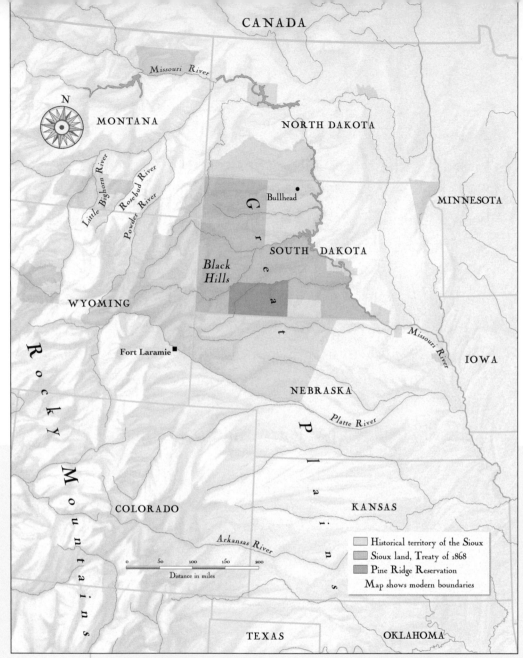

CANADA

Missouri River

MONTANA

N

Little Bighorn River
Rosebud River
Powder River

NORTH DAKOTA

G
r
e
a
t

Bullhead

SOUTH DAKOTA

MINNESOTA

Black
Hills

WYOMING

Fort Laramie

Missouri River

IOWA

NEBRASKA

P
l
a
i
n
s

Platte River

R
o
c
k
y

M
o
u
n
t
a
i
n
s

COLORADO

KANSAS

Arkansas River

| 0 | 50 | 100 | 150 | 200 |

Distance in miles

☐ Historical territory of the Sioux
☐ Sioux land, Treaty of 1868
☐ Pine Ridge Reservation
Map shows modern boundaries

TEXAS

OKLAHOMA

This map shows the original land claimed by the Sioux in light yellow, the land remaining to them after a treaty in bright yellow, and the reservation where many Sioux went to live in tan. The territorial lines were flexible and were frequently ignored by Indians in search of game. However, it is clear that the Sioux were very quickly dispossessed of most of their land.

Author's Note on Sources

The two main works on the life of Sitting Bull are *Sitting Bull: Champion of the Sioux*, by Stanley Vestal, and *The Lance and the Shield: The Life and Times of Sitting Bull*, by Robert M. Utley. The Vestal book is older, and the author was able to interview many people, both whites and Indians, who had known Sitting Bull. However, he chose to tell the story from the Indian viewpoint. The more recent book by Robert M. Utley attempts to be more objective. For younger students, there is Elizabeth Schleichert's *Sitting Bull: Sioux Leader*.

Schleichert, Elizabeth. *Sitting Bull: Sioux Leader*. Berkeley Heights, NJ: Enslow Publisher, 1997.

Utley, Robert M. *The Lance and the Shield: The Life and Times of Sitting Bull*. New York: Henry Holt, 1993.

Vestal, Stanley. *Sitting Bull: Champion of the Sioux*. Norman, OK: University of Oklahoma Press, 1932.

INDEX

About the Author

James Lincoln Collier has written many books, both fiction and nonfiction, for children and adults. His interests span history, biography, and historical fiction. He is an authority on the history of jazz and performs weekly on the trombone in New York City.

My Brother Sam Is Dead was named a Newbery Honor Book and a Jane Addams Honor Book and was a finalist for a National Book Award. *Jump Ship to Freedom* and *War Comes to Willy Freemen* were each named a notable Children's Trade Book in the Field of Social Studies by the National Council for Social Studies and the Children's Book Council. Collier received the Christopher Award for *Decision in Philadelphia: The Constitutional Convention of 1787*. He lives in Pawling, New York.